To Simon,

with all good wishes,

Morley's Laws
of Business
and Fund Management

CW01551670

Ian Morley

This book is dedicated to my late father, Alfred Morley.
Not a day passes without him in my thoughts.

Ian Morley

Published by Ian Morley

Publishing partner: Paragon Publishing

© Ian Morley 2014

The rights of Ian Morley to be identified as the author of this work have been asserted by him in accordance with the Copyright, Designs and Patents Act of 1988.

ISBN 978-1-78222-072-5

Book design, layout and production management by Into Print

www.intoprint.net

+44 (0)1604 832149

Printed and bound in UK and USA by Lightning Source

Preface

Ian Morley, one of the founders of the hedge fund industry, takes no prisoners in this book. The cartoons, laws and narratives are simultaneously profound and tongue in cheek.

Ian sees the comic and absurd side of investment, and exposes falsehoods and arrogance that have perpetuated for too long.

This is just great fun to read. It challenges the opaque language and pretensions of much of the fund industry, and provides common sense insight while leaving you with smile on your face.

A must read, and a rare opportunity to learn and to be entertained at the same time.

Mary Buffett
Co-author of The Tao of Warren Buffett and author of Buffettology

Acknowledgements

I would like to thank my good friend Yanky Fachler who edited this book and constantly reminded me that if I didn't write faster, it wouldn't come out before 2016. I did and it has.

To Lyndsey Posner, who always manages to both cut and improve anything I write.

And to all my good friends, many acquaintances and hopefully few enemies who have all helped me along the way with advice, suggestions, good humour anddeath threats.

Subject to copyright acknowledgement I happily and willingly give you permission to use any of Morley's Laws and illustrations in your own presentations. I look forward to the day when the laws are so prevalent that I will need to write 50 new laws.

Copyright © 2014

Introduction

A colleague once asked me, "As an outsider, what is your opinion of the human race?" Ignoring the implication that I am in some way not human, I replied, "I find humans mostly absurd, particularly when the people who make money think that this feat is somehow correlated to their intellectual superiority, rather than to luck and chance."

I am someone who likes to have fun. I try not to take life too seriously. (As a Spurs fan, this is probably very wise.) In my professional life, I think it should be a capital crime to bore an audience, especially if I am the audience.

After years of being bored out of my skull as I sat through the ubiquitous and anodyne presentations that seem to populate the financial world, I started scribbling some ideas for Morley's Laws. My doodles developed into 50 laws, at which point I commissioned a cartoonist to draw appropriate cartoons to illustrate my laws. For the past twenty years, I have been using some of the laws in my presentations. I was recently persuaded to flesh out each law with added narrative, stories and observations. The result is Morley's Laws.

I hope you enjoy this book. And if I manage to get you to occasionally nod and smile in recognition over something I have written, then I will have made a net contribution to the world.

Ian Morley

Law No. 1
The Hindsight Law of Fund Management

Simulated systems with 20-20 hindsight never seem to have the same foresight.

The Hindsight Law of Fund Management
Simulated systems with 20-20 hindsight never seem to have the same foresight.

Only God and Fox News commentators know exactly what the future holds. Mere mortals have to rely on the past. And so we try and predict the future by what we think we have learned from the past. Hence the expression, "There is no such thing as history, merely historians." In theory, patterns in history can somehow help us to predict what will happen in the future. In Funds Management, some people have taken this a step - or rather a mile - further down the road.

The theory goes something like this. Opinion is free, but facts (i.e. statistics) are sacred. Everything worth knowing (apart from the results of next week's EuroMillions numbers, dog and horse winners and football results) is hidden in past statistics and numbers. These numbers form patterns that identify trends. All you need is a better model than the next person, and you too can interpret the future from the past. Opinion can be left to the idle chatter of economists and other morons. Just read the tea leaves, charts, candlesticks, heat spots, trends or algorithms properly - and you too will have the key to future riches.

This explains the proliferation of investment models that use past statistics. All these models have amazing hindsight predictive capabilities. Few, unfortunately have the same good outcomes when they are applied to the real world with our money. 20-20 Hindsight regrettably is always better than the foresight of such models. The exceptions to this rule (you know who you are) are of course immensely rich!

Law No. 2
The Law of Theoretical Systems

Everyone has a system that will not work.

The Law of Theoretical Systems
Everyone has a system that will not work.

Don Rumsfeld (the former US Secretary of Defence) is famous for quoting an ancient Arabic saying about there being things that we know we know; things that we know we don't know; and things that we don't know we don't know.

Unfortunately, most people in the world think they do know something about one thing, which they usually back up with a supporting theory. These are people who phone in to radio stations with a single sentence about their theory that they feel compelled to share, only to be ridiculed by chat show hosts who are generally one step further up the Neanderthal evolutionary chain than the caller. Out of such refined research emerge numerous systems that are then applied to markets with your money.

Like the first law, most of these systems are based on past data. They will always look good when tested historically. When you think about it, have you ever seen an untested system that didn't have good outcomes on paper? I guess they wouldn't show it to you otherwise. Actually, some of them still do - and then proceed to inform you that the market is wrong and they are right. They are the ones, naturally, who raise the most money. Everyone likes a contrarian.

Of course, most of these systems don't work when tested in live market conditions. But then again, most of the systems that were supposed to work - Euro bank stress testing, the Financial Services Authority, Securities and Exchange Commission, Gordon Brown, religion - also didn't work! Ah well, back to the drawing board.

Law No. 3
The Law of Research

The more trivial your research, the more people will read it and agree with it.

The Law of Research

The more trivial your research, the more people will read it and agree with it .

They say that nothing is certain in life apart from death and taxes. The rest is conjecture that can be refuted by observation. In fact, the whole progress of true scientific research is based on the fact that ideas are cast aside when refuted by contradictory observations. Otherwise we would all still believe that the world is flat and that the sun and stars move around the earth.

In an uncertain world, we all naturally crave certainty. Which is why most of us (not you and me of course) are afflicted with a psychological tendency to want to find truth and confirmation. We don't like doubt. Profound but meaningless research, closed-minded philosophies and most religious beliefs fall into this category.

The statement, "All men will die" is certainly true. It is also useless. Which is why so many people see it as profound. All religions pronounce that God is great. What they really mean is that our version of God is great – not yours. The same is true of closed societies such as Fascism and Communism.

Because genuine and profound research is open, transparent and challenged by others, most people prefer to follow the shallow and opinionated that purports to be deep and meaningful. For a prime example of how the trivial is lapped up by the masses, simply read a Daily Mail opinion piece.

Law No. 4
The 1st Law of Black Box Systems

The only real errors are human errors.

The 1st Law of Black Box Systems
The only real errors are human errors.

Since humans built the black boxes in the first place, human error must be to blame when they go wrong. In finance and investment, there are crudely two ways of looking at the world. One tries to understand the fundamentals of markets by looking at supply and demand, money supply, tax, psychological behaviour, the madness of crowds and other characteristics of human interaction with markets.

The other simply says that all of this information is included in the price. Understand the historic nature and movement of prices, and you can improve your chances of predicting the future. Some do this by applying statistical analysis and various factor models to the numbers - a sort of "moneyball" concept.

It's a little more sophisticated when PhDs create Black Box Systems, and a little less sophisticated when those systems turn out to be no more than a five and twenty day moving average with a few bells and whistles. The problem with many black boxes is that they are often created by people who have never traded a market in their lives. Never had a margin call. Never gone to bed at night with a sense of having their proverbials on the line. In reality, they are theoreticians, often without real experience.

In 2008, I chaired a conference of these propeller heads just at the moment when all their black boxes were failing. It was a rare moment to see superior eggheads eat humble pie in public and apologise for their losses and mistakes. For a moment, it seemed that even black boxes had humans who made errors.

Law No. 5
The Law of Statistical Presentations

Figures cannot lie, but liars can always figure.

The Law of Statistical Presentations
Figures cannot lie, but liars can always figure.

The more authoritative the source of the statistic, the more powerful your argument. For example: "95% of the people independently interviewed agreed with the position of the present government." This sounds plausible until you discover that the polling company interviewed 30 people in a town that strongly supports the government.

Another hypothetical example: "Ryanair receives fewer formal complaints than most other airlines." I don't know if this is true. I just made it up. But if it were true, it's because you have to write letters to lodge a formal complaint, whereas when they are charging you it can all be done by email. So this might be a theoretically true statistic, but very misleading if Ryanair were to use it.

If you hear that a fund manager has a ten-year track record with an average annual return of 10%, it sounds good. You may even consider investing. But you then discover that he made 100% in his first year when he managed $100,000 of his own money. Since then he has made 0% in the last nine years. His average annual return remains 10%. Another true but misleading statistic.

And here is another one: If it takes one man a year to build a house, it should take two men 6 months, four men 3 months, eight men 6 weeks, sixteen men 3 weeks, thirty two men 10 days, sixty four men 5 days, one hundred and twenty eight men 2.5 days, and two hundred and fifty six men about a day. Figures may not lie, but liars can always figure!

Law No. 6
The Law of Efficient Markets

As long as people believe markets are efficient, the more profit opportunities arise.

The Law of Efficient Markets

As long as people believe markets are efficient, the more profit opportunities arise.

Larry Hite is one of the world's best known hedge fund managers. Larry was one of the key people behind the phenomenal growth of the Mint funds which became part of the giant Man Group's global growth story. During a visit to New York several years ago, I had the opportunity to meet Larry. I asked him a question "Do you believe in the concept of the efficient market?" He looked at me for a long moment before eventually replying:

"Ian, let me tell you that it is precisely because so many people believe in the efficient market hypothesis that I am a rich man."

I know a moment of truth when I hear it. The concept of efficient markets is based loosely on the simple idea that when all information is known by everyone simultaneously, everyone will then behave with economic rationality. It is on this basis that the belief in the efficient market hypothesis is so widespread.

But as Larry Hite and most good managers know, this does not work in practice. Markets do not work efficiently. People do not behave with economic rationality.

Of course, for Larry to continue being successful, it is vitally important that most people believe that the markets do work efficiently.

Law No. 7
The 1st Law for Clients

Asking dumb questions is easier than correcting dumb mistakes.

The 1st Law for Clients
Asking dumb questions is easier than correcting dumb mistakes.

Philosophically speaking, I suppose there is no such a thing as a dumb question. A question is a question, and every question is legitimate. Practically speaking, there is certainly no shortage of dumb answers out there. This law applies to people who are buying some form of financial investment product or advice. They should always ask as many questions as they need until they are satisfied with the quality and coherence of the answers. If the answer appears to be dumb, then it makes sense to question whether you should allow your money to be managed by someone capable of giving you dumb answers.

The first question you should ask is: "Tell me what you do in one sentence." If the person selling the financial investment product cannot answer that, you need to wonder if they really understand what they do.

Never be fearful of asking a question that you fear may be dumb. Too many investors are in awe of investment managers (or at least they were up to 2008). I have long believed that it was the failure to ask simple questions and to get straight answers that led to massive but avoidable losses. Remember: if it sounds too good to be true, you can bet your bottom dollar that it probably is. There is no downside in asking why this particular too good to be true proposition is not.

Law No. 8
The 2nd Law for Clients

If you can't spell it, pronounce it or understand it, don't buy it.

The 2nd Law for Clients

If you can't spell it, pronounce it or understand it, don't buy it.

I really ought to call this the David Gamble Law, in honour of the guy who coined the phrase. For 10 years, between 1993 and 2003, David Gamble was Chief Executive of British Airways Pension Investment Management Limited, and he is regarded as one of the canniest figures in the pension fund and private equity communities.

I always loved the colourful way that David, a long-time industry friend, used to describe his British Airways job. He called it running "a large pension fund attached to a small airline." It was David who coined the "If you can't spell it ..." phrase above. I know he will be happy to have me quote him to illustrate my 2nd Law for Clients.

As the accompanying cartoon illustrates, there is still an awful lot of gobbledygook that falls foul of this law. Hedge fund folks are as bad as the IT world in preferring incomprehensible language to plain English. When I hear this nonsense, I insist that the perpetrators imagine that they are explaining this to their grandmother. (Silicon Valley actually has an annual Grandmother's Award for best start-up, judged by tech-agnostic grannies.) If the hedge fund salesperson cannot give an adequate response, and if we still can't spell it, pronounce it or understand it, then if I am doing the advising, we will definitely not buy it.

Law No. 9
The Compliance Officers' Law

When senior management is complacent about derivative positions, it's because they can't see the risks for the returns.

The Compliance Officers' Law

When senior management is complacent about derivative positions, it's because they can't see the risks for the returns.

The power in all financial services businesses is explained by the dictum: "Those who make the money also make the rules." When these same people habitually make a mess, power moves temporarily to the compliance and regulation guys – but never for very long.

Derivatives are normally a kind of financial proxy for a real asset. This may be commodities, stocks, bonds or foreign exchange. It is normally a position for the future, which means that you only have to pay a small token of the future value today. This allows you to leverage the position, thereby increasing the risk. When traders do this and make money, senior managers naturally remove any obstacles from those making the money, including compliance.

I saw this at first hand when I worked at Lehman. A delightful Frenchman had a simple foreign exchange fund that made money year in year out. Since I was nominally head of such funds in Europe, I naturally asked to whom he reported, and who controlled him. I was told by senior managers in New York that they did. When everything went pear shaped, compliance and risk were all over the Frenchman like a rash. When he was successful, everyone wanted a piece of him. Paris, London and New York. When he failed, no one claimed him – and no one was responsible.

In the immortal words of JFK: "Success has many parents, but failure is a lonely orphan."

Law No. 10
The Law of Pension Funds

God gave you two ears and one mouth. When talking to pension funds, use them in those proportions.

The Law of Pension Funds

God gave you two ears and one mouth. When talking to pension funds, use them in those proportions.

This is not a theological reflection. It is an observation of the human condition. Despite, or maybe because of the fact that we have two ears and only one mouth, we try and make up for this imbalance by talking more than listening. This is dumb. Especially when the people facing you on the other side of the desk hold the keys to some of the largest assets in the world.

Do not use your mouth to extol the virtues of your product. Instead, use your two ears to listen to what they say. Try and understand their needs. Look at their liabilities and assets. Understand their existing portfolio and be honestly reflective. Does your product meet their needs? If not, can it be adapted or made more flexible so that it adds value and helps them reduce risk? Purely oral pitches that amplify the benefits of your fund, and that are delivered in isolation of pension fund feedback, are pointless and stupid.

Pension fund managers are often paid relatively low salaries, even when compared to some junior marketing person from a hedge fund. Pension fund managers have power in place of earnings. Don't pander to them. They will sense false camaraderie. Just get to know them and listen to them. You may be surprised - they may even decide to invest with you!

Law No. 11
The Differential Law of Fund Management

Systems don't know why they make money. Discretionary managers know why they lose money.

The Differential Law of Fund Management

Systems don't know why they make money. Discretionary managers know why they lose money .

This law represents one of the interminable debates in funds management. The question is: are humans better at managing money than machines? Of course, the machines are also made by humans, so in some respects the argument is self-defeating.

As Descartes said to me only the other day: Cognito ergo sum. I think, therefore I am. This excludes a large majority of the human race, including – and maybe in particular – Arsenal fans. To those to whom the dictum does apply, it means that those whose investment decisions are based on the human mind and its ability to interpret what is going on in markets, are able to explain both why they made money and why they lost it. Strangely, amnesia always seems to set in when people are asked to explain the losses. Amazingly, verbosity sets in when people are asked to explain the gains.

Machines, black boxes, mathematical models, algorithms and other non-human investment approaches, tend to follow market data or patterns. Based on past experience, they try and predict the future. Some smart machines and models even claim to be able to learn from current activity so as to not repeat mistakes of the past. These mechanical approaches may not be capable of being in a state of Cognito ergo sum. They do think, but they are not yet what some philosophers would call conscious of themselves. Sometimes these machines make money and sometimes they lose money. They don't talk about it. Only humans do that. Unless of course you believe in Hal from *2001: A Space Odyssey*, or machines from *Star Wars*. In which case my poor sister in Nigeria needs your money....

Law No. 12
The 3rd Law for Clients

There is no such thing as a free lunch, but some restaurants are superior to others.

The 3rd Law for Clients

There is no such thing as a free lunch, but some restaurants are superior to others.

This law brings back great memories for me. The first truly great hedge fund conference outside the US was held in France. The French futures market did a deal with the French government. In exchange for paying for the upkeep of the gardens at Versailles, the leaders of the French futures market got to use the palace as a venue for private parties.

The very first event was a conference for the hedge fund industry. The party was spectacular. Actors dressed in Louis XIV costumes mingled with the guests. We ate in the long room, and the meal was brought in by liveried men carrying the food on a candlelit carriage. When the Chief Executive of the French futures market stood up to speak, to my great joy he quoted my 3rd Law for Clients.

Many a hopeful investors have been burnt because they forgot the profound truth in investing: always remember that there are no free lunches. Nevertheless, it is clear that some people are better at grappling with this adage than others. If you really want to discover the location of those better restaurants, you have to find a reliable source of information and then verify it by using some shoe leather. Similarly, if you want to find those superior fund managers, you need to do your homework.

Law No. 13
The Ultimate Law for Fund Managers

There's always an index your track record can beat.

The Ultimate Law for Fund Managers
There's always an index your track record can beat.

When I originally wrote these laws some time back in ancient history, I stopped at Law No. 13. I naively imagined that I had created a sort of 13 principles of faith. But after observing the absurd behaviour of financial markets and its participants, I decided to add a few more.

All fund managers compare themselves to some index or other. The Law of Simulated Returns states every fund manager can comfortably beat this index when not actually investing real money. Some fund managers even beat the index when investing real money. All of them, like the rest of humanity, need something to beat most of the time. That is why when the track record vacillates, they need to change the index against which they are measuring themselves. After all, why would anyone want to invest with a manager who can't beat an index?

I would go further, and boldly state that most managers do not beat their indices over time. In other words, most people are actually investing with sub-par managers most of the time. However, it makes us all feel better if we are with the winners. So losers often change the index so they look like winners. If you then stay with them, they are winners - and guess who the loser is!

Law No. 14
The 1st Law of Hedge Funds

Hedge funds are many things. Hedged isn't usually one of them.

The 1st Law of Hedge Funds
Hedge funds are many things. Hedged isn't usually one of them.

This probably should have been my first law, and is based on a spontaneous comment I made to an esteemed journalist years ago when George Soros had just made one of the greatest trades in history. He had calculated that if the pound Sterling was going to join the Euro, its price had to be kept stable in the Exchange Rate Mechanism (ERM). All the currencies about to enter the Euro would not be allowed to move more than 2.5% up or down from the fixed exchange rate. If a currency did exceed this, all the European central banks would co-ordinate activities and buy or sell currencies to restore price stability.

Soros saw that his losses would be strictly limited if any politician tried to alter the pound, since that politician was limited by the actions of the central banks. Conversely, Soros saw that his gains would be unlimited if he got it right. Soros bet against the pound, pushed it out of the ERM, and made a cool £1billion.

As a result, hedge funds moved from the obscure back pages of the financial press to the front page of the Sun newspaper. Interest rates came down, the economy grew and property values went up. Instead of being knighted, Soros was blighted by the idiot politicians and the ignorant press. If he hadn't done what he did, Britain would today be in the Euro and even more bust than it is.

Law No. 15
The Law of Value at Risk

Value at risk are models that will evaluate market risk accurately on the 364 days a year when you could work it out yourself on the back of an envelope.

The Law of Value at Risk
Value at risk are models that will evaluate market risk accurately on the 364 days a year when you could work it out yourself on the back of an envelope.

Sometimes in life, bad stuff happens. No matter how carefully you plan for it, it can still catch you unawares, at great cost. Which reminds me of the story of a very senior banker at a well known investment bank.

One morning, realising that markets do not like the unexpected, he announced to his staff: "We are trading all over the world and no one knows at any time what our risk is." Disturbed by the implications of this dilemma, the banker instructed his subordinates to find a solution.

Painfully aware that he was the boss and was only capable of understanding one thing at a time, his subordinates came up with a solution. They created a single figure that would show their big boss what the bottom line risk was at any point in time. They called this the Value at Risk model - or VAR for short.

It works every day, even though, as this law suggests, you don't need it. You are perfectly capable of working out the risk yourself on the proverbial beer mat.

Of course, when you do need it, it doesn't work. Just ask all those bankers who had a daily VAR back in 2008, and were heard to exclaim, "Oh shit!"

Law No. 16
The Law of Guaranteed Funds

Most guaranteed funds have returns similar to a US Treasury Bill with fees.

The Law of Guaranteed Funds
Most guaranteed funds have returns similar to a US Treasury Bill with fees.

The funds industry took the magical phrase Guaranteed from the world of goods and services and placed it in front of risky financial investments. The result: a miracle! You can now get a good return. At the very worst, you will get your money back. Wow, what could be wrong with that? It's a safe bet.

Savvier investors always read the small print. Because the more prosaic reality is that the cost of the guarantee was usually provided in the days of high interest rates by simply not giving you the interest on your own money and using it instead to guarantee you back over time (usually about 5 years) your original cash if things went wrong. What they did was buy something called a zero coupon bond (you get no payment, just your capital back,) and then used the interest portion to buy some options that would hopefully make a return. If they did, great. If they didn't, well, several years later you get your own money back, less their fees.

Many retail investors bought these guaranteed investments because they seemed to make sense. Some institutional investors also bought these guaranteed products, even though they made little sense beyond covering the backside of the investment officer who tried to win brownie points by purchasing them in the first place.

Law No. 17
The 1ˢᵗ Law of Due Diligence

Due diligence is properly done by investors when it is early, or by regulators when it is too late.

The 1st Law of Due Diligence
Due diligence is properly done by investors when it is early, or by regulators when it is too late.

The term due diligence has its origin in the USA. It simply means checking something or someone out thoroughly before handing your money over to them. When it's professionally done, every aspect of a funds process and management are examined in detail. The movement of cash, the level of governance, the systems used and third party providers are all closely scanned and evaluated. A low score means no investment.

In the halcyon days of financial lunacy between 2001 and 2008, many investors forgot to conduct proper due diligence. They based their investments on relationships or an image of potency, and they handed clients' money to such rogues as Madoff. Those of us that kept our heads did our due diligence and didn't invest. Others, in particular some of the major regulators, failed to do theirs. The US regulator, known as the Securities Exchange Commission (SEC), did such a piss-poor job (if you don't believe me, just read their own report into their failures) that they probably should have sued themselves if they had not been the regulator.

At the time of writing (2013), regulators the world over are still publicly closing stable doors long after the horses have bolted. I would expect little else. It will be the same next time.

Law No. 18
The Law of Benchmarks

If you under-perform the benchmark, moving the benchmark down is usually easier than moving the performance up.

The Law of Benchmarks
If you under-perform the benchmark, moving the benchmark down is usually easier than moving the performance up

Everyone in life tends to get measured against something or someone. Modesty prevents me from revealing any further personal details.

Fund managers are normally expected to do better than if you leave your money on deposit with the bank or Government. Many fund managers only get paid an additional performance fee if they beat a set benchmark. Sometimes, in low risk investments, this benchmark is no more than the return on a Gilt or US Treasury Bill. If the fund is invested in equities, the closest equity index may be selected as the benchmark. Increasingly, many benchmarks are specially created to test the manager's ability to beat them.

Of course, most managers over time do not beat their indices. That is why one of my first questions to a manager is, "Why don't I buy the index you are supposed to beat instead of investing with you?" Poor responses get short shrift.

As most managers fail to beat their indices over time, they all find it easier to lower the benchmark than to raise the performance. Watch out for this little trick. Managers who have done particularly badly and may never beat their benchmark again, often start a new fund and set a new benchmark. And so it goes on.

Law No. 19
The Law of Derivative Speak

If you use too many Greeks, you end up with a Turkey.

The Law of Derivative Speak

If you use too many Greeks, you end up with a Turkey.

In order to confuse clients and sound educated and intelligent, many fund managers prefer to use Greek rather than English. Indeed one or two of them are Greek, or have studied Classics at university.

The Greeks not only gave us great insight into how to avoid paying taxes and how to borrow billions from the Germans and not pay it back, they also gave us the foundations of democracy, itself a Greek word. They gave us terms like Alpha (first) and Beta (second). If you are wondering why financial folk don't simply use the terms first and second, it's because it wouldn't sound as clever. Over time, all these Greek alphabet (yes, that is alpha + beta) and numerical terms have undergone slight changes in meaning. Today, we all understand what is meant by an Alpha male, (whether human or beast.) It is the leader, the best, the first. Now all fund managers are in pursuit of Alpha returns. It is the holy grail of fund management. Most fund managers of course only deliver Beta (market or second rate returns). Other obscure terms include Delta, Gamma and Theta. To make things even more complicated there are even different definitions as to what these words mean in financial markets.

There is no need to use Greek jargon, especially since other professions also use the same jargon to mean something different. It becomes so complicated that if you use too many Greeks, you do end up with a turkey (the Anglo Saxon definition of a mess.) My mixed metaphor is not designed to cause offence to either Greeks or Turks, who I know have a great fondness for one another.

Law No. 20
The Law of New Products

If the product is really new, you have six months before the competition start to copy you.

The Law of New Products
If the product is really new, you have six months before the competition start to copy you.

Imitation maybe the sincerest form of flattery, but it's an unwanted compliment if it's a direct hit to your bottom line. If you really have some form of new Intellectual Property, then a good lawyer (new oxymoron?) should be able to get you some period of protection from direct copying - otherwise known as theft. If you do not have IP protection, the competition will quickly disaggregate or reverse engineer your product and come up with their own version. In the world of IT, the time to move from industrial hubris to embattled nemesis can be quite short. Just look at Nokia and Blackberry as examples.

In the world of finance, it can be even more difficult to maintain an edge. You can buy or sell, borrow or lend or some derivative of these. Truly new or creative normally means large profits for the seller and large cost for the buyer until the rest of the market has worked out what you are doing, at which point they begin to attack your margin of profit.

Sometimes everybody gets into the game together and mass delusion takes place. This happens about every ten years. The securitisation of Sub-Prime debt (collecting rubbish together and pretending it has value) was the most recent example. It's easily spotted because the "juvenile scribblers" start to talk about a new paradigm. At this point I suggest you get out and run for the hills.

Law No. 21
The Law of Averages

Being average over time is superior.

The Law of Averages
Being average over time is superior.

Statistically, I am never sure if this is correct or not. My guess is that it is.

However, averages can be dangerously misleading. Let's say you borrow £10k from your mum, call yourself an investment manager, and start using a 5- and 20-day moving average to trade the Tasmanian Greasy Wool Market. If by chance this coincides with a one-year period when the market was going up, you might turn your £10k into £20k - a 100% return on your money. If during the next nine years you moved from £20k to, well, nowhere, and you stayed at £20k, you can still claim to have achieved an average annual return of 10%. On such statistical illusions are track records built.

However, if you are truly capable of delivering steady returns over a long time period, and if your mean (average) and mode (middle number of count) are close to the same, then this steady - dare I say soporific - return is actually close to the holy grail. Why? Because consistent return without too much volatility is what most investors are looking for.

So, being truly average over time, is in fact superior. Few managers actually grasp this simple argument. They always want to be seen as better, best and deliverers of Alpha. If they consistently managed average over an extended period, then they would probably be doing better than most.

Law No. 22
The Law of Intuition

A good feeling is not measurable, nor is it always treatable.
That does not necessarily make it wrong.

The Law of Intuition

A good feeling is not measurable, nor is it always treatable.
That does not necessarily make it wrong.

This is almost a clichéd statement. In this case, that's positive. Not an unqualified positive, but still a positive. Sometimes you just have a feeling (good or bad) about markets or a business opportunity. It can be difficult to measure, but this does not mean you have taken leave of your senses. By all means use all your senses, and then try and get all the facts. Go with your feeling. If time allows (not always the case), trust your gut feeling - but verify all the facts and references.

The most compelling ideas may instead turn out to be fraudulent. The most compelling proponents can turn out to be the most appalling fraudsters. They are skilled in making you believe in them and their get rich ideas. That is how they get rich, and how you get poor. Your gut feeling, or the gut feeling of your other half if you have one, is often the best gauge of people and their proposals. My gender experience is that women sense issues or problems far more quickly than men do. Instead I usually take a trusted female colleague along with me to meet people I am thinking of doing business with, in order to benefit from her independent feedback.

First impressions and feelings are often correct – but not in isolation. Common sense and due diligence must confirm what you feel - otherwise all you will feel is sick!

Law No. 23
The Law of Risk

Risk is reduced by non-correlated diversification. So are the returns.

The Law of Risk

Risk is reduced by non-correlated diversification. So are the returns.

I was once asked by a colleague ahead of a presentation if I would drop the last four words of this law: "So are the returns." I reluctantly agreed. After all, I told myself, it was his diversified, non correlated fund that we were presenting.

Risk control is one of those areas that has moved from common sense to a state of near theology in modern fund management. A welter of academic research in the 1960s said in a nutshell: If you make up your portfolio with a number of different asset classes, e.g. stocks, bonds, commodities, FX, emerging markets etc., and then refine this by trying to pick the ones that don't all move in the same direction at the same time, i.e. the so-called non-correlation effect, then you reduce the risk of the overall portfolio.

Sounds great. Very sound advice. The only problem is that many of these non-correlated assets end up reducing returns as often as they reduce risk. And it can get worse. In 2008, it did get worse, when many investors discovered that the only thing that went up in a down market was the correlation of their non-correlated assets. As Pharaoh said before he entered The Red Sea in pursuit of the Israelites: "This wasn't supposed to happen!"

Law No. 24
The Contrarian Law of Fund Management

Good opinion is not influenced by the view of lemmings.

The Contrarian Law of Fund Management
Good opinion is not influenced by the view of lemmings.

It's not that the crowd gets it wrong. They just get carried away by the mass of other lemmings doing the same thing. Ergo, they must be right. Blind enthusiasm is no substitute for brains. The psychology of the crowd overtakes the reality, and takes markets both too high and too low.

One of the smartest managers I know (let's call him Hugh Hendry of Eclectica to safeguard his anonymity) never follows the herd, and never reads the views of juvenile scribblers. He takes his own counsel from his own observations, and draws his own conclusions. This is true contrarian thinking. Hugh is one of the very few great managers out there who operate this way. It's not easy. It can be lonely going in the opposite direction of the lemmings.

Another manager like this is Richard Edwards. Richard has applied chaos theory to markets, which allows him to observe the lemmings in action. By following the behaviour of the crowd, he is often able to accurately see where markets are getting compressed and may soon break out. He predicts when and what to buy, and has been remarkably accurate in his predictions. He writes a narrative, but only in order to put the findings into an economic context for those of us that like reading stories. This should not be seen in itself as an explanation of market behaviour. Richard is telling us what will happen, not why?

Law No. 25
The Law of Losses

Losses are the markets' way of dealing with Fund Managers' egos.

The Law of Losses
Losses are the markets' way of dealing with Fund Managers' egos.

Successful fund managers can be pretty egotistical. Anyone who can consistently make money in financial markets is either very talented (rare) or very lucky (more common). Either way, most people discount the luck part and deify the skill part. Success, wealth and importance are easily confused with great knowledge and wisdom.

Take the guys behind Long Term Capital Management (LTCM). Not happy enough with the sobriquet "Big swinging Dicks" that had attached itself to some of them in former roles they came to dominate the fixed income arbitrage market in the late 1990s. With a Nobel Prize winner on board, they were so confident (read: arrogant)   about their systematic way of trading short-term against long-term US Treasuries that they really believed they had invented the financial equivalent of the Holy Grail.

Except that they hadn't. It all went horribly wrong. Rates that should have moved closer together actually moved apart. The "dash for cash" caused the price of short-term Treasuries to move up much faster than anticipated. The result: one of the largest hedge funds was wiped out. Maybe even some of them were humbled for a day or so. However, men with such obvious talent seldom remain deflated for long and some were soon up and running again looking for new investors to join their latest offering.

Law No. 26
The Law of Karma in Fund Management

When you can keep your head when all around are losing theirs,
it's probably because you don't understand the situation.

The Law of Karma in Fund Management
When you can keep your head when all around are losing theirs, it's probably because you don't understand the situation.

Kipling was absolutely right. Sometimes in life, the best response when others are panicking is to keep calm. As the world saw when Captain Sully successfully landed his stricken plane on the River Hudson in January 2009, if you are the pilot of a plane and you know how to land the plane on water in an emergency, calmness is an admirable trait.

In financial markets, calmness can be a sensible response when you insist on retaining your considered position against the opinion of the crowd. However, it can also be very expensive when you get it wrong.

In theory, it is always possible that you are right and the market is wrong. The danger is that if you try and hold on to a losing position for too long, the losses will wipe you out.

Being calm, relying on your karma and celebrating your contrariness is one thing. Being plain obstinate is another. You may keep your head when all around you are losing theirs. Maybe, when your plane has been hit by a bird strike, you really do know how to calmly land your plane on water.

Then again, you may not have a fucking clue!

Law No. 27
The Law of Business Travel

The total sum of e-mails, faxes, mobiles and video conferencing has led to more business travel, not less.

The Law of Business Travel
The total sum of e-mails, faxes, mobiles and video conferencing has led to more business travel, not less.

I suppose I am living proof of this. I travel more today on business than I ever did before, despite all the modern forms of ether communications.

The reason is simple. Very few deals or business relationships are created in the absence of true human contact. I have never done a deal without meeting the other party face to face, without establishing a sense of chemistry. Of course, this can also have a reverse outcome. You meet someone face to face, and discover that the reality is a disappointment compared to the picture you created over many years through phone or email contact. Anecdotally, this is also the usual outcome to most internet dating meetings. We too often struggle in reality to match up to our perceived persona.

I have an iron principle: I will never do a deal or even due diligence on a potential business partner without a face-to-face meeting. Those old and trusted supplicants, food and wine, are still valid and still work. Get the person out of the office. Get to know them. What they like, where they live, what their hobbies are. Are they charitable? What do their family do? All good old fashioned stuff, but it still works. You can never achieve this over an ether connection, no matter how sophisticated.

Law No. 28
The Law of Statistics

The volume of statistics is not a persuasive argument in the absence of an intelligent thought process.

The Law of Statistics

The volume of statistics is not a persuasive argument in the absence of an intelligent thought process.

When it comes to statistics, politicians are even more egregious than those of us in finance. Substituting statistics in the absence of policy or an intelligent thought process is the hallmark of the modern politician. We hear the claim, "We built 500% more hospitals during our time in office than the last sorry bunch." That of course may mean that there was one hospital, and they built five more. While the present government has built ten hospitals, which is twice what the former bunch built, but less in percentage terms. Anyway, you get the idea.

I did a lot of business in Japan in the late 1980s and 90s. The Japanese were convinced that funds management was an industrial science like car manufacturing, not an art. They would data mine to the third or fourth decimal point. They were convinced that if they had enough data, they could re-engineer the process and do it themselves, only better. They couldn't and they didn't.

Baseball fans and train spotters are geek gatherers of statistics. And however anal this pursuit might seem, I have to admit that these two groups sort of get it. They know that knowledge of statistics makes a huge impression on the other members of your table at a supper quiz. (Q: How fast was The Mallard travelling when it broke the world steam locomotive speed record? A: 126 mph.) But this statistical adeptness does not give them any greater knowledge.

In a world overrun by the cosmic numbers of data and statistics on the Internet, too few people have realised that most of this noise detracts rather than adds to the sum of human knowledge.

Law No. 29
The Law of Bull Markets

Even a fool can make money in a rising market.

The Law of Bull Markets
Even a fool can make money in a rising market.

Never in the history of financial services has so much been taken by so few from so many. When markets go up, they are called Bull markets. When they go down, they are called Bear markets. These terms have entered modern parlance. We speak of people being bullish (positive about something) and bearish (cautious or fearful about something). When markets are going up, they tend to do so for prolonged periods of time. When they fall, this is often shorter but also sharper. With the exception of cynics and curmudgeons, most people prefer markets to go up.

So do fund managers, as they make money for their clients - but much more importantly, they make money for themselves. When markets remain bullish for long periods, two phenomena can be observed. Most fund managers become very arrogant, and cannot differentiate between the rising market and their skill. Dangerously, they confuse the two. Worse, every amateur investor suddenly thinks they have become stock picking gurus. They become instant dinner table bores, ready to match their equally boring friends who think they have the gift of property investing.

It is true that even a fool can make money in a bull market. When you hear all the fools chortling in chorus about their gains, it's probably time to sell before you become the last fool left.

Law No. 30
The Law of Active Managers

If active managers believe they add value, they should short their benchmark and leverage their positions.

The Law of Active Managers

If active managers believe they add value, they should short their benchmark and leverage their positions.

Oops! I suspect that this requires a little more explanation, this time in plain English. Passive managers believe that it is not possible to beat the market. They just buy the index and charge you less. Active managers, of course, are always convinced that they can indeed beat the market.

So here is a really good way to put their belief in themselves to the test. Most fund managers will normally measure their performance against a benchmark. This benchmark is normally some kind of index. The challenge therefore is to tell them that if they are that good, they should take the benchmark and sell it short – which means selling something you don't own in order to buy it back (hopefully) at a lower price. At the same time, they should increase (leverage) the position of the stocks or assets they do own. This will eventually demonstrate if they really are capable of using their skill to beat the market.

If indeed they are using their using their skill, the rewards will be multiplied. Of course, if they are not, it is the losses that will be multiplied.

It is with regret and sadness that I have to inform you that very few – if any - active managers have ever agreed to take me up on the challenge. I wonder why?

Law No. 31
The Law of Human Views

The market doesn't behave like a human being, but it gives a price for the current sum of all human beings.

The Law of Human Views
The market doesn't behave like a human being, but it gives a price for the current sum of all human beings.

It is a frustrating paradox that fans of the school of behavioural finance would like us to believe that the markets are just a reflection of human behaviour. If that were the case, most psychologists would not just be bonkers, they would be very rich. Or is that psychiatrists? Maybe both. While I personally probably err on the side of behavioural finance theory, it just doesn't work when you need it to. The problem is: Who the hell knows what humans will do? Some, as Warren Buffett points out, are "greedy when others are fearful. And some are fearful when others are greedy."

The problem is that it is not only human beings who influence markets. Politicians can and do also influence markets. They are forever trying to pick winners and support or weaken currencies, subsidise grain or metal prices, fund infrastructure or housing projects and other things that will create false values, while trying to do good - and more importantly, while trying to get re-elected.

And just to add to the general chaos, machines and mathematical models are also programmed to trade at different times and in different ways. Of course, we could describe all this as the sum of human creation and behaviour, but this doesn't make things any easier or any clearer. In an absolute sense, the market provides pricing. It may be fair and reasonable, or it may be mad. Madness certainly rules from time to time. The price is there, but who knows whether the value is there. That's why there are buyers and sellers at most price levels.

Law No. 32
The Law of Diversification

Too much diversification will result in profit neutral positions.

The Law of Diversification
Too much diversification will result in profit neutral positions.

Here is a tale about another great fund manager, John Henry - perhaps more famous today for owning the Boston Red Sox and Liverpool Football Club. He once agreed to look at the portfolio of a young manager who had been running after him at a conference that John and I were attending. He looked at the portfolio, and said it was perfectly diversified – and was profit neutral! The point was that when you over diversify, you may reduce risk, but you may also reduce any chance of profit.

This is another of those conundrums. Risk is controlled by diversification - and so are returns. Fees are a constant, irrespective of gains and losses. If you over-diversify (rule of thumb - in excess of 40 managers, and even 20 is probably too many), all you do is trade off the returns from one for the losses of another. You, of course, still have to pay them all. Diversification makes theoretical sense, but over-diversification becomes counter-productive.

To paraphrase the great Warren Buffett, diversification is what you do when you don't know what to do. Buffett is essentially saying that diversification is the standard fallback position. It works by spreading risk, but often fails to deliver return. Return only happens when you know what you are doing with a concentrated portfolio.

Law No. 33
The Law of Consultants & Senior Management

Consultants are brought in when senior management knows the answer but doesn't want to make a decision.

The Law of Consultants & Senior Management
Consultants are brought in when senior management knows the answer but doesn't want to make a decision.

I have to tread a bit carefully. So many of my laws are about consultants, and I do not want to antagonise them en masse. When I first started jotting down these laws back in the 20th century, I was a hedge fund manager. Today I am a consultant.

My experience of consultants over the years, with certain exceptions (modesty prevents me from including myself in this category), has not always been totally positive. Generally, I have seen too many senior executives being scared of making the decisions that are painful. Governments are even more scared of making painful decisions. Unlike senior executives, who are not subject to the democratic process, governments can be more easily voted out of power.

It is always a safe option to bring in expert consultants, tell them what you are trying to do, pay them enough money, and hey presto! They will come to the same difficult conclusion you would have come to yourself. And they will present you with your ideas embedded in a thick tome. This allows you to very reluctantly agree to go along with this hard choice, because – after all – it was an outside consultant (and not you) who suggested it. There is now a convenient scapegoat.

Law No. 34
The Law of Consultants and the Moment of Truth

Consultants tell you things you already know but don't want to face.

The Law of Consultants and the Moment of Truth
Consultants tell you things you already know but don't want to face.

Only a complete moron or a downright naive executive ever hires a consultant to tell them something new, something they don't already know. Consultants are there to confirm what you know but for whatever reason you can't or don't want to face. Consultants are there to tell you the blindingly obvious, often in obscure language, in great detail and at great expense. These consultants are naturally highly valued.

Companies are very good (or should that be very bad?) at ignoring the obvious. They may be losing market share because they have become arrogant and lazy. They may be relying too much on past ideas, old models or tired brands, and are no longer capable of delivering the goods. Most managers, apart from those who are truly self-delusional, are probably aware of this. But facing such unpleasant truths means having to do something about it, and that could prove unpopular.

When they get the consultant to tell them the unpalatable truth, there is a collective sigh of relief. Purged of their uncertainties, the senior executives now have a clear understanding of what they need to do. And what they need to do is avoid their moment of truth at all costs. So they proceed to do nothing at all until it's too late. The history of the decline of great companies is replete with such stories.

Law No. 35
The Law of Consultant Avoidance

Most consultant costs could be avoided if you listened to the people who work for you.

The Law of Consultant Avoidance

Most consultant costs could be avoided if you listened to the people who work for you.

This is probably the most basic and profound of all my consultant laws. The very best consultants and the most knowledgeable people are right under your nose. They are the people who work for you. They see all the mistakes, deal with all the nonsense and bureaucracy, know why products and services fail, have an intimate understanding of the market and clients, and know the comparative strengths and weaknesses of your company's products or services vis-a-vis the competition. Naturally, they are ignored! Why listen to the people who work with you on a daily basis, when you can bring in people who don't, and get their advice at great cost?

In rare cases, senior management do ask their workforce what they think, and then reject it because they don't like the answer. This type of conversation can sometimes take place at the annual Christmas party, when senior directors are strategically seated at the tables of the minions. If they are lucky, they get to sit with a secretary they have ogled all year. As the level of alcohol consumption increases, employee fear dissipates, and they begin to treat the directors with expletive-rich opinions about what should be done. The result is often acute embarrassment all round and, in some cases, the search for a new job in the morning.

It is a sad but observable fact of business life that many senior executives are deaf, blind, arrogant or a combination of all three. They fail to recognise that the best consultants are there every day at the office or factory.

Law No. 36
The 1st Law of Conferences

If you mix up networking and neckworking, you may end up with drawdowns in the wrong place.

The 1st Law of Conferences
If you mix up networking and neckworking, you may end up with drawdowns in the wrong place.

Few people actually attend conferences in order to listen to the speakers. The exception is when I am speaking, of course. Most people attend in order to network, to catch up with colleagues and competitors, to eat and drink together and try and sell things to one another. At academic conferences, it is ideas that are being traded. Fund conferences try and sell funds and the extra bits like administration, custody, location and systems.

Some conferences are truly tedious, with the great and the good congregating in not so great and good city centre hotels. Many of the speakers, especially in finance, are poor. Other conferences are held in beautiful locations with spas and great views and facilities. These conferences are called boondoggles, because the organisers get it. They realise that this is an unpaid for holiday courtesy of your company for your private benefit. Speeches and panels are kept to a minimum so that delegates can just have a good time.

In some conferences, delegates get carried away by the wine and location and confusedly mistake someone's interest in selling them something for an interest in themselves. When this happens, neckworking replaces networking, with a resulting drawdown in the privacy of their rooms. Unfortunately, in finance conferences, delegates are 90% male. So unless you swing both ways, there is a paucity of such nocturnal activity.

In my next life, I am coming back as a straight man in the fashion business.

Law No. 37
The 1ˢᵗ Law of the Press

It is easier to check the quote first than to deny it later.

The 1st Law of the Press
It is easier to check the quote first than to deny it later.

The trade press is usually on your side. The general press often takes the opposite approach. If truth is often the first casualty of war, be very wary of the press. Always be courteous, because they can make powerful enemies. Some journalists are knowledgeable, and some may even rank as truly gifted. Unfortunately, they are the exceptions. All journalists are supposed to subscribe to the theory that facts are sacred and must be checked, while opinions are just that, other people's views of the facts. This subtle distinction is often unclear.

If a journalist asks you for your opinion on some subject, ascertain whether this is on or off the record. Make clear whether they can quote you directly (which significantly increases your chances of getting into print) or whether they can just attribute your comments to an un-named source

Very few journalists allow you to edit their piece. They regard this as trespassing on their territory. However, I will always insist on seeing my quotes in context, before they go to print. It is easier to check the quote first than to deny it later. It is very easy to get tripped up in the eye-catching but often misleading headline written by a sub-editor in order to catch the eye of the reader. I know someone, let's call him Bloggs, who gave a slightly negative opinion on the short-term direction for the Euro. The headline read something like: "Bloggs: German hegemony continues to dominate Europe." You can imagine his embarrassment when this appeared just as he was about to go into a meeting with his German client. Oh dear!

Law No. 38
The 2nd Law of the Press

Just because it's in The Economist does not make it true.

The 2nd Law of the Press
Just because it's in The Economist does not make it true.

If *The Economist* was writing a lead article about Genesis, the first book of the Old Testament, it might read: "God's mistake was that, in the absence of demonstrable evidence of his existence, he created miracles without evidencing them in a form that is comprehensible to the rational mind. Had God taken this logical approach as this journal suggested at the time, then the rest of history could have been spared religion."

I naively used to believe the veritas of *The Economist* articles concerning subjects of which I knew little, until I realised that articles on subjects about which I was knowledgeable were sometimes not so accurate in key respects. *The Economist* has never had a great liking for derivatives or hedge funds, and regularly featured negative articles about these subjects.

Several years ago, I read an article by an un-named journalist (sadly, all *Economist* journalists have no named bi-lines) which quoted some research from a US-based professor in order to make a negative point about futures fund management. My familiarity with the professor's work made me question the quote, so I called the professor. He did not know that *The Economist* had used part of the material he sent them at their request. He also did not know that they moved the decimal point in the article.

I naively tried to do battle. When I eventually found the journalist, he declared himself not guilty of the offence. Well, guilty of the decimal point error, but too arrogant to accept any change in his opinion. My "Angry from Tunbridge Wells" letter to the editor was completely ignored. All my subsequent letters of complaint about The Economist article on Hedge Funds have apparently been filed in the waste paper basket. *The Economist* in my view likes the sound of its opinion more than contradiction.

Law No. 39
The Law of Transparency

Transparency is a bit like virginity - vastly over-rated and of no practical use when you need it most.

The Law of Transparency
Transparency is a bit like virginity - vastly over-rated and of no practical use when you need it most.

The demand for transparency has become a modern mantra. Investors demanding transparency really want to see every position every day that the manager may hold in his fund on their behalf. This obsession with transparency is often ill thought through. What are investors going to do with all this data, especially if they are in a fund that only allows them to exit once a month, often with 30 to 90 days advance notice? Knowing the positions is a bit like receiving an accurate forecast of an oncoming hurricane when you are mid-ocean in a small sail boat. You know the facts, but they cannot affect the outcome.

Transparency can even be damaging. The most sensitive positions a manager holds are his shorts, not his longs. Shorts have an unlimited risk profile, longs can only fall from the current price to zero. If knowledge of these shorts becomes public (you may have a big mouth), it can undermine the value of the position as others get to hear about it and try and push the price up to test the resolve or bank balance of the manager. In this sense, the demand for transparency is of no practical use when you need it most.

If you really can do something with all the numbers and data to improve the risk control of your position, by all means ask for transparency. If you can't, don't bother. It will just confuse you. A bit like virginity, it will probably just embarrass you in mature financial company.

Law No. 40
The 1st Law of Alpha

Alpha is what all active managers seek to deliver. Beta plus costs is what most actually deliver.

The 1st Law of Alpha

Alpha is what all active managers seek to deliver. Beta plus costs is what most actually deliver.

If you are literate like me iz, you can read and write and possibly even count. To make financial services folk seem clever, we prefer to use Greek and Latin instead of English. A bit like dogs that lead the pack from the front, we like to refer to ourselves as Alpha. In financial terms, this means our objective and impartial view of ourselves – our ability to return more to our investors than is generally available from the market, which we call Beta.

There is a problem of logic here. Most managers consider themselves Alpha types, otherwise why would you invest with them? Simply buy an index (Beta) and achieve the average return at a lower cost. However, it is logically not possible for most managers to be better than the average. This small but salient observation is normally ignored as investors follow fame rather than sense. In reality, only a few managers can beat the average, and even then it's not always the same ones or for a long time.

Alpha doesn't remain Alpha for too long when arrogance moves in. So, most managers tend to deliver Beta (the market average over time) and not Alpha. Even the Beta is not free, since brokerage and manager fees are charged. The result, sadly, is that most managers deliver Beta plus costs.

Law No. 41
The Law of Indexation

Only Beta can be indexed. Indexation of Alpha is a contradiction in terms!

The Law of Indexation
Only Beta can be indexed. Indexation of Alpha is a contradiction in terms!

We have already discussed the terms Alpha and Beta, so I can assume that you are an expert.

I was a panellist at a hedge fund conference in Paris where we were discussing the development of investable hedge fund indices. Try and stay awake, please. A fellow panellist waxed lyrical about his company's latest hedge fund index as a way to capture the Alpha without the high fees, lack of transparency or liquidity. When I suggested that his offering was something between alchemy and sophistry, he first had to look up these words in the dictionary. He didn't seem very happy.

I then told the audience of several hundred that if Alpha is better than Beta, it must be logically impossible to index Alpha. By definition, if you can index it, it must be Beta. Therefore, only Beta can be indexed, and indexation of Alpha is a contradiction in terms. I had to re-read the last sentence a few times to understand it but it is in fact true. My fellow panellist tried to hit me. I sympathised with him. So would I have liked to hit me had our positions been reversed.

Sophistry and alchemy have long been the hallmarks of many financial products and offerings. Remember: If it's special and limited, it's rare and called Alpha. It cannot then become packaged and sold to everyone. Yet this is still what people try to do with most Beta products. The simple yardstick is: Beta products are sold. Alpha products are bought.

Law No. 42
The Law of Leverage

Despite the proliferation of multi-leveraged mortgages, few people understand financial leverage when it goes against them.

The Law of Leverage
Despite the proliferation of multi-leveraged mortgages, few people understand financial leverage when it goes against them.

Many of us have mortgage or credit card debt. This is a form of leveraged debt. Like a lever is used to ease a wheel nut, we use a small amount of money to leverage a large amount of money we don't possess. We take out a mortgage to buy a home that we could not otherwise afford. We then have to repay the debt over a period of time.

During strong markets, banks lend to anyone. Their logic is that either they will be repaid, or property prices will always go up. If all else fails, the bank can just take back the property and sell it to someone else. When everyone gets drunk on this property spiral, the banks not only lend to prime (good) credit risks like you and me, but to bad credit risks (sub-prime customers.) Alchemists and bankers tried to persuade us that sub-prime was better than prime, by taking all the sub-prime rubbish and selling it as a bundle of toxic waste happily AAA rated by the dim-witted rating agencies.

We all understand leveraged debt - until the property market crashes or we can no longer pay our debts. We all then become innocents, incapable of understanding the consequences of our decisions. Help is always on hand. A sub-life form known as ambulance-chasing lawyers is instantly available to sue the banks and credit card companies for misleading us into such financial traps. Most of the money you make this way goes in fees to the lawyers protecting your innocence.

Law No. 43
The True Law of Risk

Without risk there is no return.

MORLEY'S LAWS OF BUSINESS AND FUND MANAGEMENT

The True Law of Risk
Without risk there is no return.

In Law No. 12, I pointed out that there are no free lunches in finance. Every investor wants a return greater than what is laughingly called the risk free rate. The risk free rate is normally a rate that you get for lending money to the government to waste on the discredited notion that governments are good credit risks. If you doubt this, just ask the opinions of the Greek, Spanish, Portuguese, Italian and Irish investors.

To achieve a return greater than this ludicrous risk free rate must by definition incur risk. To overcome this, many sellers of financial service products wrap their offerings in blankets with nice names attached: "Low risk," "Protected," "Guaranteed" and the like.

The simple truth is in all investments there is risk. The theory (not always the practice) says the greater the risk you take, then the greater the reward you seek. Seeking return without risk is a fool's paradise and best avoided. The sensible thing is to decide how much risk you can take or want to take for an expected level of return.

Anything else is just wishful thinking.

Law No. 44
The Quant's Law of Risk

Risk can be modelled.

The Quant's Law of Risk
Risk can be modelled.

The term quant or geek is usually a noun applied to a person who can count above ten without taking off their shoes and socks and who understand a bit more about maths and engineering than the rest of us.

These quants often think risk in finance is a bit like building a bridge or plane. They know it will come under stress from time to time, but if you build it strongly enough, it will withstand this stress. They use the tools of engineering and maths to test their theories by making complex models that tell them how much strain the financial model can take under duress. The problem is that these models are far more successful when applied to the world of engineering where the risk factors are well known but less varied than the behaviour of crowds.

The science is less easily transferrable than most quants realise. As they perfect their models, they tend to get ever more complex in order to encapsulate ever increasing factors. There is little evidence that these complex models are any more robust than simple ones. The only thing that is not in dispute is that the only people who understand the complex models are the quants that created them. It still baffles them when the world and its chaos are not controlled by their models.

Sadly, what works for bridges and planes (they also both fall and fail from time to time) does not work when applied to the result of mass human behaviour in markets. Which doesn't stop the quants from trying. When they fail spectacularly, as in 2008, they even mumble the odd but rare word of apology.

Law No. 45
My Mum's Law of Risk

How much can I lose?

My Mum's Law of Risk
How much can I lose?

Of course my mum was always right. I gather that this is also true for all women. I once heard some sound advice from a future father-in-law to his prospective son-in-law. "For a good and lasting marriage, always remember to say 'You're right, I'm wrong, I'm sorry.'" Very sound advice. They got divorced after two years because he was also married to Goldman Sachs, who are a very tolerant investment bank.

There has been a proliferation in funds management of what are known as risk adjusted returns, a sort of measure of the levels of risk compared to the levels of return expressed in complex ratios with odd sounding names like, Sharpe, Sortino, Information, Omega and so on. In fact, my mum's common sense approach is still the best place to start in any understanding of risk. "How much can I lose, or how much am I prepared to lose before cutting a loss?" This is what behavioural psychologists now call regret risk. Would I regret losing this amount? No, if it's £1 on the lottery, the reason we all do it. But yes, if we bet the house on the lottery, which is metaphorically what poorer people do. That is why it's a voluntary tax on the poor for the benefit of the rich.

If you keep your losses under control, you will have less of them, and that will allow you to make more in better times. My mum intuitively understood this. Even in her nineties, she would lecture me on the benefits of being careful and not taking too many risks. Her dad had lost his business and fallen on hard times, so she knew about the harsh lessons of loss avoidance. If my mum had been running the banking system, none of this mess would have happened in the first place. And if my dad had been allowed to run the war, we would have beaten the Germans by Christmas.

Law No. 46
God's Law of Risk

Man plans and God laughs.

God's Law of Risk
Man plans and God laughs.

Although the evidence is not totally convincing, I suspect that there maybe even a higher and more powerful life force than my mother. Some people refer to this as God. Manchester United fans like to think that Eric Cantona was God, but this cannot be true as he was French. If God does exist, he would of course be English.

I always enjoy the debates between closed minded scientists and even more closed minded clergymen. The scientists ridicule the notion of an omnipotent God, and reduce most religion to superstitious nonsense at best, and to manipulative power of organised religion for its own ends at worst. The religious hit back by saying that science may explain how, but religion and God explain why.

As a lifelong Spurs fan, I struggle to believe in a God that can allow a team as completely ghastly as Chelsea to steal the European Championship, while ending up below Spurs in the league. Whatever you think about God, karma or some higher life form is perfectly normal. My cats know which way round. So does my dog, and they both disagree. What we all do know is that there is something out there that laughs as we plan.

To lower the tone of the debate by a few notches, shit happens, sometimes referred to as a black swan event. When the things we don't know we don't know come and bite us in the bum, we find that all our well thought through plans were all for nought. As that famous philosopher Mike Tyson once said, "everyone has a plan until they get punched in the face."

While specifically apt for most risk planning in investments, this law is also somewhat like Einstein's quest for a general law. It holds true for most things in our lives.

Law No. 47
The Law of Companies in Trouble

When the cost accountant cancels the FT and/or when the CEO orders the corporate jet.

The Law of Companies in Trouble
When the cost accountant cancels the FT and/or when the CEO orders the corporate jet.

None of Morley's Laws are theoretical. They are all based on real experience. I have experienced this particular law on more than one occasion. In one company, I experienced both parts, albeit with some small time interval between the jet being ordered and the Financial Times being cancelled.

These are always signs of fear at the bottom of a business cycle or excess at the top. While at Lehman, I remember a note going round saying that all senior executives were sufficiently rewarded and could therefore buy their own FTs each day. Of course we could, but that was not the point. The writer of this memo might just as well have said the company has financial problems and is making cutbacks to save itself. This was in fact many years before Lehman collapsed. When American Express bought Shearson Lehman, as it then was, this was another one of those marriages made or destined for hell. Another company I knew got into financial trouble when Senior Directors would only fly by private jet. I should have realised then that the writing was on the wall. This was about two years before the company crashed.

The most absurd version of this was when Lehman bought expensive art and wine while at the same time it cut back on staff. You could stare at great art works in the lobby and corridor, get sloshed at lunchtime on excellent claret, but you had no budget for a secretary in the days when other people typed our letters.

Law No. 48
The Law of Academic Research

Most academic research in business and fund management is used in the way a drunk uses a lamppost: more for support than illumination.

The Law of Academic Research

Most academic research in business and fund management is used in the way a drunk uses a lamppost: more for support than illumination.

I would never suggest that academic research can be bought. As everyone knows, academic research is undertaken by disinterested scientists and researchers who are seeking truth and knowledge for the general advancement of humanity.

Some people believe that dog food endorsed by a guy in a white jacket holding a test tube, quoting from scientific research that two out of every three dogs prefers Joey dog food to starvation, is backed by impartial and non biased findings. Such people will probably also believe that pigs can fly.

Commissioning such research to help you sell your product, service or fund can be many things as far as marketing is concerned however, it is rarely objective academic research. If you are an idiot, you will let them do it impartially and then publish the findings irrespective. Few do this. Most guide or direct the researchers to the outcome they are looking for. Dictators throughout history know the power of how you phrase the question. "Would you like me as your ruler or would you like to rot in prison for ever?" This personifies the Putin approach, rather than the Obama approach which says: "Vote for me, I am better than the other guy."

Most companies let the researchers do their work and then pick out the good bits. Statisticians are really expert at this. They can make the numbers sing. They can statistically prove anything, and often do. For example, almost every fund manager wants 2008 out of their track records. By the beginning of 2014 they will be able to show a five year track record excluding 2008. All you need to do is carefully choose your start and end points and then that will give you the result you need.

Law No. 49
The Cynic's Law of Business Strategy

The only constant synergy is the amount of dislike one profit centre has for another.

The Cynic's Law of Business Strategy
The only constant synergy is the amount of dislike one profit centre has for another.

If large companies were efficient, boutiques wouldn't exist. Large firms always talk about group synergy and brand awareness. Group synergy does not exist. It's all in the mind of senior management and their PR agencies.

In the dim and distant past, I was a Director at Lehman Brothers. I ran what would today be called Alternative Investments in Europe for them. From time to time, senior US heads would fly over to the UK and even take me on jollies around the European offices, where they were wined and dined by the local MDs and made to feel very important - even more important than the self-importance they granted each other via their impressive and high-sounding titles.

I always had a big mouth and suicidal career tendencies when working for these big monoliths. I remember at one such gathering of Lehman notables, when less notables like me were asked about group synergy, I answered truthfully that there is no group synergy here apart from the hate that one profit centre has for another. Fortunately, they all laughed out loud, convinced that this is another example of British humour. It was. Sick, ironic, and clearly lost on our American bosses.

Law No. 50
The Law of Business Plans

Most business plans in hindsight could have been short-listed for the fiction awards.

The Law of Business Plans

Most business plans in hindsight could have been short-listed for the fiction awards.

My favourite business plan was conceived by my 4-year-old son, who wanted to sell apples from our garden to neighbours at £1million pound an apple. When I suggested that his mark up may restrict sales, I got a bollocking from the wife for discouraging him.

Many of the business plans I have seen since lacked the reality of my son's. Whether it is a disruptive new technology or a widgets factory, they all have income and cost graphs showing costs ascending more quickly than income in the first year. By year two, the business goes cash flow positive, with income now exceeding cost. In year three all previous costs have been covered and the business moves into absolute profit and no debt. By year five we are all billionaires. And to make this happen, I just have to invest a few thousand or hundreds of thousands of pounds. There is usually an accompanying narrative that explains the genius of the idea and the even greater genius of the entrepreneur making the business case.

Now, I am a glass half full type. I get excited and drawn in by people's business dreams. But I only have finite resources, so I must first conduct due diligence. Most business plans grossly underestimate the time it will take and costs involved. Doubling both is a useful rule of thumb. Too many people fail to adequately research their market.

My rule of thumb for business plans is: A smart idea presented by smart people.Focused, full time, self invested and not expecting you to subsidise their former lifestyle. If you can tick those few boxes, you are off to a good start.

Lightning Source UK Ltd.
Milton Keynes UK
UKOW04f2101200914

238893UK00001B/10/P